DISCARDED BY THE
URBANA FREE LIBRARY

On Being Me

On Being Me

A PERSONAL INVITATION TO PHILOSOPHY

J. David Velleman

Illustrations by Emily C. Bernstein

PRINCETON UNIVERSITY PRESS

PRINCETON AND OXFORD

Published by Princeton University Press

41 William Street, Princeton, New Jersey 08540

6 Oxford Street, Woodstock, Oxfordshire OX20 1TR

press.princeton.edu

Data LCCN 2019047501 (print) | LCCN 2019047502 (ebook) | ISBN 9780691200958 | ISBN 9780691200965 (ebook)

LC record available at https://lccn.loc.gov/2019047501

LC ebook record available at https://lccn.loc.gov/2019047502

British Library Cataloging-in-Publication Data is available

Editorial: Matt Rohal

Production Editorial: Debbie Tegarden

Text Design: Leslie Flis

Production: Erin Suydam

Publicity: Katie Lewis

Copyeditor: Gail K. Schmitt

Jacket art by Emily C. Bernstein

This book has been composed in Sabon LT Std text

Printed on acid-free paper. ∞

Printed in the United States of America

10 9 8 7 6 5 4 3 2 1

For Eli, Jamie, and Micah

For Bubbie and Zeydeh, my parents, and Tim

Contents

Preface

For me, philosophy begins with puzzlement about what it's like to be a person. I want to know why being a person seems the way it seems, given that it often seems to be something that, upon closer examination, seems impossible. Unavoidably, I have thought about these puzzles in the first person, the perspective from which I am acquainted with how being a person seems. I've spent almost forty years trying to figure out why being a person seems like *this* to *me*.

Throughout those years, I have written in the impersonal voice of a professional student and teacher of philosophy. I've approached the puzzling aspects of personhood as academic exercises rather than personal conundrums. Here I present some of my ideas as reflections on those conundrums, setting scholarship aside and writing in the first person.

I am not claiming independence of the philosophical tradition. Readers familiar with the discipline will recognize the ideas of authors beginning with Heraclitus and extending up to my current colleagues. Among my contemporaries or near-contemporaries, the most influential have been Elizabeth Anscombe, Michael Bratman, Daniel Dennett, Gareth Evans, Harry Frankfurt, Gilbert Harman, Christine Korsgaard, Iris Murdoch, Thomas Nagel, Derek Parfit, John Perry, and Bernard Williams. Among historical figures, I have learned most from Aristotle and Kant. There are also crucial bits of John Locke and William James that I could not have done without. Outside of philosophy, my sources include Sigmund Freud, Prescott Lecky, William Swann, and Kurt Vonnegut. Citations to these authors appear throughout my academic publications, some of which are listed in the Readings at the end of this volume.

These first-person reflections do not extend to every aspect of personhood. In particular, they do not address my relations with other people, a topic that does not lend itself to the introspective method I adopt here. (I discussed

interpersonal relations in an earlier book titled *How We Get Along.*)

As I explore my personhood, my thoughts become convoluted—unavoidably so, because a person is a convoluted sort of thing to be. The self-awareness that is distinctive of persons entails not just awareness of oneself but also awareness of one's self-awareness, which opens into a house of mirrors where the philosophical explorer can quickly become disoriented. My hope is that the reader will not be deterred by an occasional stubbed nose.

I originally thought some of the more convoluted parts of the book would require schematic diagrams as an aid to comprehension. But when I chanced on Emily Bernstein's online sketchbook, I saw that she could create artwork that was both illustrative of the philosophy and delightful in itself. I invited her to read the manuscript and draw the thoughts it suggested to her—thoughts of the sort I hope it will suggest to any reader.

Academic philosophers who read this book will say, "But there are no arguments!" Let me be the first to say it: There are no arguments. There are only observations of what being a person is like for me and speculations as to why it might be like that.

Most of these observations and speculations have appeared in my academic publications, sometimes supported by more or less formal arguments. For many years I thought the arguments were meant to convince the reader, but then I found myself oddly unconcerned when few if any readers were convinced. I finally realized that I have all along been reporting on personal explorations, composing dispatches from an examined life. My main hope has been that these dispatches will be of interest even without a demonstration that they are true of persons in general.

I am aware of, and embarrassed by, the similarities between the inner monologue of this book and that of Descartes in his *Meditations*. Pretending to be a twenty-first-century Descartes would be ridiculous. I prefer to think that I am simply accepting his challenge to philosophize from the inside out.

On Being Me

1

Being Glad I Was Born

I owe it to my parents.

Not that they conceived me for my sake: they didn't know it would be me. In fact, there wasn't anything to know, no identity waiting to be embodied in a child yet to be conceived.

So maybe I don't owe my parents anything for my existence. They just tossed the gift of life into the void, hoping a recipient would materialize.

Maybe my life wasn't even a gift. It didn't make me better off than I previously was or otherwise would have been. Nor would I have minded the alternative. Even now, the thought of never having existed doesn't bother me.

The thought of not going on existing is another matter.

2

Wanting to Go On

Given that I exist, I want to go on.

I usually assume I'll go on existing just as long as there is breath in my body. But then I wonder whether my body might outlive me, if dementia scrambles my memory or a coma blots out my consciousness. As I contemplate such prospects—well, I don't even know whether they *are* prospects for me rather than the absence of a prospect altogether. Looking ahead, I can't see into such radically altered states, and so I wonder whether I would still be there, even though my demented or comatose body would still be breathing.

Some would say the reverse—that I will outlive my body, in the form of an immortal soul. But even if I had a soul, its survival would matter to me only because, in that case, it would be me. What matters to me is to go on being me.

But what is that?

As soon as I focus on the question, it seems to evaporate. What could my going-on-being consist in except the going-on-being of a body, a soul, or some other thing that I am? Yet no matter what sort of thing I consider myself to be, I find myself indifferent to the continued existence of that thing except insofar as its going on would amount to my going on, and so I am back where I started, wondering what it is for me to go on being. What is this condition, "being me", that a future dementia patient might or might not inherit along with my body or soul? Without knowing that, I can't know what I am relying on my body, my soul, or anything else to perpetuate.

Setting aside dire possibilities, then, I need to ask, with respect to a denizen of the future who definitely *is* me, what exactly his being me *is*.

If that is the question, though, the answer is trivial: being me is just like being here, which is not a way of being at all.

"Here" refers to a place—as I write, 5 Washington Place, New York, NY, 10003, USA. The word refers to

5 Washington Place because that's where it is being used. But it doesn't describe 5 Washington Place *as* the place where it's being used; it just picks out that place as if by pointing, like an extended index finger.

Similarly, "me" just picks out the person using it, like a thumb mutely poking its owner in the chest: it doesn't describe that person at all. So if the question is what it takes to be me, the answer may be that there is literally nothing to it.

But what about the person who will wake up in my bed tomorrow and put on my clothes? How can *I* call *him* "me", given that I can't just poke him with an inwardly pointing thumb?

Can't I, though? I can certainly poke myself right now, and he will be the same person as the one I'm poking.

Yet when the question is whether I'll continue existing, the continued existence of this person seems no more decisive than the continued existence of a body or a soul. I can care about going on being me even if I wouldn't go on as the same person. Parting company with this person is harder to imagine than parting company with this body, but I can imagine it—have imagined it, in fact, although

I was sleeping at the time. For I once dreamed that I was Socrates, and when I woke up, I didn't describe it as a dream in which I didn't exist. I was definitely there in the dream, albeit as Socrates. Apparently, then, I can imagine being someone other than David Velleman while still being me. Similarly, some people claim that they remember past lives in which they were other people—fourteenth-century knights or nineteenth-century suffragettes.

Of course, my being Socrates was only a dream, and people who claim to have lived past lives are mistaken at best. These experiences don't show that being a different person is really possible. But they do show that it's not only conceivable in the abstract but imaginable in concrete detail—which is enough to show that my continued existence can matter to me whether or not it would also be David Velleman's. Going on being as someone else would be better than not going on at all—wouldn't it?

But what am I thinking when I think of myself as a different person?

Let me start with an ordinary case of continuing to exist. At the moment, I am working in my office, and I have just now thought, "I'll keep writing, and in an hour I'll quit for lunch." Clearly, I was expecting to go on being me for at least an hour, given that I planned what "I" would do then.

But the references of the two pronouns in my plan ("I'll keep writing ... I'll quit") didn't perfectly coincide.

The first "I" referred to me as I thought it; the second "I" referred to a person quitting and going to lunch in an hour. Of course, the person going to lunch will be the same person as the one who was making the plan as he wrote. But is that why I referred to him as "I"—because of our being the same person? I wasn't thinking about who I was or who he will be, and so I don't seem to have shared the pronoun with him on the basis of our sharing an identity. Why, then, did I use "I" for him?

Well, my thought was a plan to quit work in an hour, and a plan has to be deposited in memory and retrieved later, when the time to act on it arrives. The plan won't just sit in my memory unchanged. Over the next hour, an occasional glance at the clock will update it, so that in half an hour it will be, roughly, "I'll quit in half an hour", and then "I'll quit in 10 minutes", and then "I'll quit in just a moment". These updates will not be newly minted decisions; they will just be revised versions of the original plan, re-expressed from the perspectives of successive times. Over the course of the hour, the plan will count down until it reaches the equivalent of zero—namely, "now", as in "*Now* I'll quit". Only then will it be ready to act on.

I suppose the plan could initially have said what "he" would do in an hour—"he" meaning the future subject who will find himself with an updated version of the plan designating the time to act as "now". But then the pronoun would also need to be updated, from "he" to "I", since "Now *he* will quit" would leave him wondering "Who, me?" And although temporal updates are useful in measuring out the hour between now and lunchtime, the personal update would serve no purpose. I might as well install the first-person pronoun in the plan from the start, given that I'm delegating the planned action to a future subject who will be the referent of that pronoun when the time arrives. For who else can enact my plan but the thinker of its final update, in whose mind the countdown will have reached zero? And how else should it then refer to him but *as* its thinker, hence in the first person? That future subject is someone I can think of in the first person because I can frame first-personal thoughts of which he will be the thinker when it's time to act.

I'm tempted to say that the pronoun is like a hook that I'm casting forward in time, hoping to snag the relevant person by addressing him from his own point of view, as if pointing to him with an inward pointing thumb. In fact, though, there is no particular person I'm hoping to snag. The relevant person will be whoever I manage to snag with the pronoun—whoever ends up thinking, "Now I'll quit," thereby intercepting the first-person reference.

It's not that I'm counting on him to enact the plan because he'll be me; rather, he'll be me because he's the one on whom I can count to enact the plan.

This use of the first person is like my use of the second person in the voicemail message on my phone. The message "You have reached the mobile phone of David Velleman" is addressed to whoever ends up hearing it and thus occupying the position of its audience, addressable as "you".

I suppose I could have used the second person in my plan: "If it's noon and you're still working, then quit for lunch." I might even have written a reminder on a slip of paper: "Take your lunch break at noon." But a plan is not exactly like a written reminder. The person who was meant to act on the written reminder would be the one reading it at noon, the note's audience, addressable in the second person ("your lunch break"); the person to whom I must delegate execution of my plan will be the one thinking it at noon, addressable in the first person ("I'll quit").

In short, "I'll keep writing, and in an hour I'll quit" uses the pronoun in two different ways—first to pick out the person thinking it now, and then to pick out the person who will remember it and be thinking it later. In this case, they're the same person, but I wasn't relying on their being the same person when I used the same pronoun for both of them.

When I update my plan in ten minutes, I may have a memory of experiencing this very moment, as I sat here working, with the clock at 11:00, a sentence unfinished, and 12:00 still an hour away. The memory won't show the subject of that experience: it will just show the things experienced—the clock at 11:00, the unfinished sentence, the thought of lunch. But it will implicitly represent those things as experienced by a subject, the unseen viewer and hearer and thinker of the remembered sights, sounds, and thoughts. So there will be two subjects involved: the subject remembering this moment, and the subject it is remembered as being experienced by. One will be the subject *of* the memory, the other will be the subject *in* the memory. If I then say, "I remember when I saw the clock at 11:00," the first pronoun ("I remember") will refer to the former, external subject, while the second ("I saw") will refer to the latter, internal subject.

Although these subjects are in fact the same person, the grammar of the statement doesn't require that they be the same. It's like the grammar of "I dreamed I was Socrates", which referred to two different people. The first "I" ("I dreamed") referred to David Velleman, the subject who actually had the dream. But the second "I" ("I was Socrates") didn't refer to David Velleman. I didn't dream that David Velleman was Socrates — as if Socrates was reincarnated in 1952 and renamed. Lost in a dream, I wasn't even aware of being David Velleman, only of being Socrates.

No, the second "I" referred to the subject *in* the dream —the one who was living in the world of the dream, according to the dream itself. And he was a different person from the subject *of* the dream, the one who dreamed it and, now awake, was using the pronoun to identify who he dreamed of being.

But how can I use the first-person pronoun to pick out someone other than me, the person using it?

Well, the dream must somehow have intimated that Socrates was its internal, dreamworld subject. And the only way for that intimation to show up in the dream was to show up in the mind of that subject—the mind of the dreamworld subject—where it must have been the thought "I am Socrates". What I must have dreamed, in other words, is inhabiting that world while aware of being Socrates.

Whenever I see or hear or think something, in fact, I am aware of being the one who is seeing or hearing or thinking it. The experience includes awareness of myself as the subject of that experience. That self-awareness is expressed by the first-person pronoun when I report what "I see", "I hear", or "I think". The person picked out by that pronoun is the internal subject of sight, hearing, or thought, the one represented as its subject by the self-awareness embedded in the experience itself. That internal subject is usually the same as the subject actually having the experience, the external subject—but not in the case of dreams. A dream can represent the world as being experienced by someone other than the actual dreamer. It can pick out a different internal subject by supplementing the dreamed "I see", "I hear", or "I think" with a dreamed awareness of who "I" am. I could say, "I dreamed, quote, I am Socrates, unquote," pantomiming the quotation marks with two fingers crooked on either side of my head. But I transpose the direct quotation into indirect speech (from "dreamed, quote, I am Socrates unquote" to "dreamed *that* I was Socrates"), retaining the first-person pronoun to indicate that I dreamt of Socrates from his first-person point of view.

Enough about the dream. I brought it up only as an analogy for my memory of what I saw, heard, and thought at 11:00. Fully spelled out, the state of mind I'll remember is that of seeing, hearing, and thinking those things while aware of being David Velleman. But that last, additional bit of the memory will go without saying.

What won't go without saying is the self-awareness that's embedded in the remembered sights, sounds, and thoughts: it will be expressed with the first-person pronoun when I go on to describe what I remember that "I saw", "I heard", or "I thought". That pronoun will be used by the subject *of* the memory, the one remembering, to denote the subject *in* the memory, the one by whom the sights, sounds, and thoughts are remembered as having been experienced. I naturally assume that those two subjects are one and the same person, and so having described what I remember that I saw, heard, or thought,

I won't bother adding who I remember that I was aware of being. But the assumption that we're the same person can be denied in other cases, as in reports of my dreams.

ch

Calling the internal subject of a memory "me" expresses more than his self-awareness as subject of the remembered experience; it also expresses an aspect of what it's like for me, the external subject, to remember that experience.

When I recall visiting the Empire State Building with my grandfather sixty years ago, my memory of the view over the parapet seems less like a mental image than a window through which I am even now viewing the original scene. I seem to be looking through that window from a position slightly above and behind my remembered self, as if looking over the shoulder of the six-year-old me. And I can just about imagine climbing through the memory-window to become that six-year-old self again.

ch

I now understand why people claim to have lived past lives as other people. They have a mental image of chaining themselves to a railing outside Parliament, or strapping

on a suit of armor, and that image passes through their minds spontaneously, as if directly delivered by memory rather than cobbled together by imagination. So they think that the image derives from an actual past experience, and that the internal "I" implicit in it refers to an actual person. The natural way to report what they take to be passing through their minds is "I remember when I was a suffragette" or "I remember when I was a knight in armor"—statements that would be true if the images were recovered from the experiences of an actual suffragette or knight.

Of course, those statements are false when spoken in the twenty-first century, because the speaker's mental image is not a record—not even a faded or doctored record—of an actual person's experience. The speakers are imagining that they were suffragettes or knights and mistaking that image for a memory. But when I say, "I remember when I visited the Empire State Building with Grandpa," I am describing mental images recovered (in faded or doctored form, perhaps) from the experiences of an actual six-year-old boy who visited the Empire State Building with his grandfather. Looking over the six-year-old's shoulder to share his visual experiences is only an illusion, but the fact remains that his experiences really are the source of my memory images, and I am therefore remembering the first-person awareness of a real viewer of a real scene, as I report by saying that I remember what "I" saw.

Similarly, if I could retrieve stored mental images of a fourteenth-century knight's experiences—a big "if"—I would be correct in claiming to remember when I was that knight. I'd be casting the pronoun backward in time to snag the source of my memory image, whoever he might have been.

So much for the past "me". It's still only 11:10 and I am looking forward to seeing the clock at 12:00, when I can go to lunch. Of course, I can't literally see that experience in advance. So in what sense can I "look forward" to it?

Oh. Here is something I *really* need to figure out. For it's precisely what I want in wanting to go on being: I want a future that I can look forward to.

I don't mean that I want to be clairvoyant. Though I sometimes have no clue what some future occasion will be like, my inability to envision it doesn't prevent me from looking forward to it. And even in that case, I'm not completely unable to envision it; for I can envision that my experience of the occasion will include the memory of having had no clue what it would be like. I can envision thinking, in light of my then-remembered cluelessness, "At last I know what it's like!"

I usually imagine a future experience in that way, as including a memory of how I imagined it. Although I can easily imagine being surprised by the next person who appears at my office door, I can't imagine being surprised by its being a particular person, because my image of the experience naturally includes my remembering having hereby imagined it and hence being prepared for it to be him or her. I thus imagine that this very image will have survived in my memory to meet its fulfillment in experience.

Similarly, when I try to imagine the experience of quitting work, I imagine it as including a memory of this attempt to imagine it, retrieved by its subject for comparison with the reality. I regard my mental image as if it were permeable and I could pass through it into the imagined scene, leaving the image at my back as a memory of what I imagined. Though I won't actually pass through the image, of course, I will indeed remember it and even be able to follow it as a guide to my behavior. I can imagine

having lunch in the park, so that the future subject having this image at his back will be guided to the park at noon.

My anticipatory image of that future experience also includes, along with the anticipated sights, sounds, and thoughts, the self-awareness of their subject *as* their subject—his "I see", "I hear", and "I think". Those first-person pronouns refer not to me as I anticipate the experience but to him, the internal subject of the anticipated experience. And if (as I anticipate) he remembers having hereby anticipated his experience, those first-person pronouns will end up pointing to him from his perspective, like an inwardly pointing thumb.

As in my plan to quit for lunch, then, I am casting those pronouns forward to snag the subject of the experience in which they are remembered. There is no particular person I'm hoping to snag. The relevant person will be whoever I manage to snag with the pronoun—whoever ends up taking the "I" in the remembered image as pointing to him, thereby intercepting the first-person reference.

So whereas a memory represents the experience of the subject who was its source (whoever he was), a forward-looking image represents the experience of the subject who will be its recipient on the intended occasion (who-ever he will be). And just as I will describe the memory as representing what "I" experienced in the past, I now describe the image as representing what "I" will experience in the future, thereby expressing, as part of the anticipated experience, the subject's awareness of being its subject, which must be expressed in the first person.

Could that be all there is to going on being me—the future existence of a subject whom I can call "me"? Surely that can't be worth caring about. After all, what's in a pronoun?

Yet it turns out that many important aspects of my life involve forward-looking thoughts of just that kind. I often desire things as palpably gratifying this very desire, which thus anticipates surviving to be gratified. In hoping for things, I hope to receive them with the open arms of this hope; in fearing things, I fear facing them on legs trembling with this fear. In fact, most of my feelings about the future are feelings I wouldn't have if I thought I would no longer have them when the time arrived. If I want to have chili for lunch, I want to have it only if I still want it at lunchtime, so as to experience the fulfillment of this desire. What I really want, in fact, is to experience the meal *as* what I hereby envisioned and wanted all along. For I want my satisfaction to be heightened by the memory of having wanted chili for what will then have been the last hour.

These feelings are investments in the future, in the sense that they envision surviving until they can be resolved, discharged, paid off. And in envisioning their future resolution, they don't identify the person who will experience it; they pick him out merely as the subject of that experience. In wanting that "I" enjoy a bowl of chili at noon, I am referring to the subject who will still be feeling this hunger at noon and will remember, "I've been wanting this all morning." And I'm referring to that subject—and thinking of him as referring to me ("I've been wanting")—irrespective of who either of us may be.

Of course, desires and emotions needn't anticipate a resolution in order to be strong and significant. When I think about the future lives of my grandchildren, I have strong and significant feelings about events that I may not live to see.

But my feelings about those events are not preparatory to them, and so they don't involve me in the future. When I want something envisioned as gratifying this desire, I am already preparing for it, as if sounding the opening notes of a musical phrase to which I already anticipate a closing cadence that will be heard as resolving this remembered opening, or as if beginning a story in anticipation of an ending to be read as resolving this remembered beginning. In the present moment, then, I am already involved in something larger than the present; whereas in wanting long and happy lives for my grandchildren, I am only a bystander. It's not just that I won't be involved in their later lives; I am even now uninvolved in them, in virtue of having no access to preparatory desires or emotions about them.

So the connections of anticipation and memory by which I can think of someone as "me" in the future also enrich my present, by giving me even now a role in something larger than a momentary existence. Those connections give me *a life*—not just a stretch of going-on-being but something with phrasing and cadences, beginnings and endings.

If someone else in the future really could remember living my life—could intercept the first-person references in mental records of my plans, anticipations, and experiences—then I would go on being even if David Velleman did not. I don't know how that could happen, but I do know what would amount to its happening. If I knew it was going to happen, I could even make plans for what "I" would do in his or her shoes, *as* him or her. So I am not essentially David Velleman, because my existence could conceivably come apart from his.

This realization gives me a better understanding of the age-old belief in souls. The idea of my soul is the idea of a self that floats free of my mundane existence as a person. It's as if our ancestors, having discovered that they were not essentially who they were, felt the need for something else to essentially *be*—a personal essence.

Yet the idea of having a soul doesn't do justice to my independence of my mundane identity. For as I realized at the outset, going on being me is not the same as being the same soul—or being the same thing, for any kind of thing whatsoever. Our ancestors went astray, not just by inventing the soul as the thing they essentially were, but by thinking that they essentially were *things* at all.

I am not a thing, not an entity of any kind. In the narrowest sense, I am the subject of thoughts, feelings, and experiences occurring now, and I am linked by first-person reference to past and future subjects who I remember and anticipate being. More broadly, I am an entire train of those subjects, coupled together by my remembering being them and anticipating their remembering being me. And I will go on existing so long as that first-personally connected train of thoughts and experiences continues.

3

Fearing the End

I've gone on being for sixty-six years, and now I'm starting to worry about running out of time. That's why I'm dismayed at the approach of birthdays, each to be followed by fewer returns of the day.

Yet if my next birthday is approaching, it must be getting closer to something. What is it getting closer to?

It isn't getting closer to the present, since the present is a particular day (March 3, 2019) whose distance from my next birthday (November 14, 2019) never changes. Those two days are and always will have been 256 days apart, never closer. What's getting closer is rather the event of my birthday's *being* present. But that event is approaching only because it will occur on November 14, which is getting closer, and that's what I'm trying to explain: how does that day get closer?

Let me try a different metaphor—say, that the present is like a spotlight that shines on each day in succession. What's moving in this case is the spotlight, creeping up on my next birthday, which is stationary. Movement requires a change of location, and the way the spotlight moves must be that it shines on different days. All at once? Of course not. It must shine on different days *on different days*, shining on each day on that day, moving at the rate of one day per day. So each day is illuminated for its own duration, and in this respect there is no difference between days. If anything changes, it must be—what?—it must be which day is illuminated *today*.

And now I've come full circle for the second time. For which day is today? It's the day that's lit up by the spotlight. But every day is lit up for a day. Today must be different because of *when* it's lit up. (Repeat *ad inf.*)

The problem is that the word "today" is like "here" and "me", referring in this case not to the place at which, nor to the creature by which, but to the day on which it is used. The present seems to move because the word seems to be moving from one day to the next. But the word isn't really moving; it's just being used repeatedly, each use occurring on only one day. That string of utterances is like the string of cars that make up a train, each car sitting on its own section of the track: "today"–"today"– "today"– .... The fact that a train occupies one section of track after another, with one perfectly similar car after another, doesn't mean that it's moving. Movement requires the very same thing to occupy different locations at different times. The problem with "today" is that utterances are events, each of which can occur at only one place and time.

Ah, but every one of these utterances issues from *me*. Here I am, saying it today; there I will be again, saying it tomorrow. I seem to be laying down those utterances along a track that stretches from past to future. So my sense that the future is approaching must be like the sense that my destination is approaching as I ride a train. It's actually me that's approaching the future, not vice versa. In any case, *something* is moving.

Wait a minute. In order for me to be moving through time, I would have to be one and the same thing from one day to the next. Didn't I recently conclude that I'm not a thing at all?

Let me start over again, using the railroad analogy. The fact that a train occupies successive sections of track doesn't mean it's moving, if it occupies those sections with successive cars, each of which sits on a different section. The question, then, is whether it's the whole of me or different segments of me that occupy different days, or indeed different moments.

It certainly isn't different spatial segments. I have spatial segments only in the sense that my body has them, and all of them are present at every moment—the crown of my head, my waist, the soles of my feet, occupying different regions of space. But couldn't there also be different segments of me that occupy different intervals of time? There was a time when I was an infant; at a later time, I was an adolescent; then an adult. Someday (not yet!) I'll be an old man. These different slices of me seem like different cars on a train, hitched together across

the extent of my lifetime, which extends not in space but in time.

The young me and the old me are different slices of me because they are separated in time, just as my crown and my soles are different slices of me because they are separated in space. Spatial separation is measured by the three dimensions of width, height, and depth; time is just another dimension, a fourth dimension, in which things are related not as higher and lower, or leftward and rightward, but rather as earlier and later. Just as my head is higher than my foot, the young me was earlier than the old me.

If I exist over time in virtue of having different segments at different times, then I'm like the stationary train that has different cars on different sections of track: I don't move through time but merely extend along it. The alternative would be for me to be wholly present—all of me—at every moment of my life. Considered spatially, of course, all of me—all of my body—*is* present at every moment, a complete human being from head to foot. But given that I exist in different regions of the fourth, temporal dimension, what exists of me in any given temporal region is not my whole temporal extent, from junior to senior, but only one of those segments.

To be sure, my segments are all parts of a single person. But they make up a single person in virtue of the connections between them, like the couplings that join separate rail cars into a single train. In the case of my spatial segments, the connections are forged by my skin, my muscles and tendons, my nervous and circulatory systems. I've already noted the connections among my temporal segments: they're the connections of memory that enable me to think of past and future subjects simply as "me".

In thinking of them in the same way I think of my present self, as "me", I seem to be thinking of one and the same thing. In reality, though, the reason why I remember and anticipate experiences as had by "me" is not that their subjects were or will be one and the same thing; it's rather that I can use the first-person pronoun to pick out the internal subjects of memory and anticipation, and that I seem to look back and forward, through those mental images, to past and future scenes. The resulting appearance of perfect self-sameness through time is what produces my sense of traveling through time, which in turn produces my sense of time's going by. In fact, though, I'm referring to the subjects of successive segments in a temporally extended sequence of mental states, each regarding not only himself but also the others as "me". In each mental state, the subject feels as if he has just arrived from the past and is about to depart for the future. In reality he's not going anywhere: he exists only for a moment, retrieving thoughts and mental images recorded by the subjects of past mental states and recording thoughts and images to be retrieved by the subjects of future states.

That's ridiculous.

Either I am moving through time or it is moving past me—one or the other. We're not both standing still. If we were, nothing could change. I couldn't so much as walk down the block; I'd just be a sequence of earlier and later segments standing on successive squares of the sidewalk.

Even if I'm not a thing that remains the same thing from one moment to the next, I insist that I have a personal perspective that travels with me, to different places at different times. It's not a standpoint fixed to a single location around which objects are perceived as arrayed in space; it's not a standpoint fixed to a single moment around which events are perceived as arrayed in time; it's a standpoint fixed to *me*, perceiving events and objects as making up a single outspreading, ongoing world. If objects and events at various places and times are to hang together from that point of view, it cannot be divided up into segments; it has to be a unified, persisting perspective, as it certainly seems to be. I'm sure of it.

But no. That unified, persisting perspective is what I've been trying to identify from the very start: it's what makes me "me" to me across time, connecting me to past and future selves. And I've been able to disassemble it into plans, memories, anticipations, and feelings rooted in different moments but linked in such a way as to create a semblance of unity, and hence a semblance of movement. There only seems to be movement where in fact there is none.

I'm forced to conclude that the passage of time is an illusion, albeit an illusion that's impossible to dispel. I'm not *going* on being at all; I'm just *being* at different moments with different segments.

So the end of me is not a cliff toward which I am constantly hurtling; it's merely a segment of me with nothing beyond it in time, just as there is nothing of me above the crown of my head or below the soles of my feet. I don't mind having top-most and bottom-most spatial parts—having endpoints in space—so why do I mind having an endpoint in time?

Well, I do have reasons for minding it. One reason is that my temporal extent may not reach far enough to include a future witness of particular events—my grandchildren's graduations and weddings, for example. I want to be there, represented by future segments who inherit the unfinished stories and musical phrases to be completed by those celebrations.

In that respect, these desires are not at all like my desire to have chili for lunch. A bowl of chili isn't something that I want to survive in order to eat; it's something that I want to eat if I'm still around and wanting it at lunchtime —otherwise, never mind. My grandchildren's graduations and weddings, however, I want to be there to see— otherwise, I *do* mind, though of course I won't then.

But then what's the point of wanting to exist to see them? My desire to see them anticipates its own gratification, but if that gratification never occurs—if my temporal extent is cut short—the never-to-be-gratified desire will already be in the past, never to meet with felt disappointment. Or, rather, it will meet with felt disappointment only if I learn of the impending end in advance, from the mouth of a physician or a news flash about incoming ICBMs. Maybe that's a reason for hoping to reach the end unexpectedly, in my sleep or even under a bus.

Or maybe it's a reason against making emotional investments in the future. I can still want my grandchildren to graduate and marry, without caring whether those desires survive to meet with gratification. It's primarily for my grandchildren's sake that I care about their reaching such milestones, anyway. I care about my own gratification only insofar as I want not only that their graduations and weddings take place but also that they include me as gratified witness. And that latter aspect of my desire entails the risk of wasted emotional energy now or severe disappointment later. Wouldn't I be better off without it?

Sometimes I manage to live without it, entirely in the moment, each temporal segment including the joy (or pain) of its fleeting existence without looking forward or back. But I always return to the felt rush of daily life, attempting merely to infuse it with drops distilled from that momentary stillness.

I have no desire to live in the moment always, at every moment, without having desires and emotions about a past and a future envisioned as mine. For as I realized earlier, those feelings give my present existence meaning, as a note in an extended phrase or an episode in an extended story. I just need to find a way to experience my going-on-being lightly, as meaningful but not entirely real.

4

Regretting What Might Have Been

My life story could have been different.

As a boy I hoped to be a dancer when I grew up. At some point in my forties, I realized that I was still hoping. I enrolled in ballet class—not because I still hoped to *be* a dancer but just in order to dance. Yet I still had, and still have, a fantasy of an alternative universe in which I am a dancer.

Do I regret having become a philosophy professor? Do I wish that I had become a dancer instead?

Me? As I am now, in my sixties? Certainly, the person I am now couldn't be a dancer. But maybe I could have been a retired dancer with a career in dance to look back on, if only .... Well, I'm not sure how to fill out that "if". If I hadn't been discouraged from studying dance as a child? And then if I had majored in dance at college instead of philosophy? And then?

Even if I could fill out those hypotheticals, I'm not sure I would be regretting that *I* am not that other person. My doubt is not whether I could be that other person while still being me as I am now. I'm setting aside the qualities I have now and considering the qualities I would have had if I had taken a different path from a young age. The question is whether the person who took that path would be me, only different.

Despite the differences, he and I would share a lot: we would share the same childhood up to the point where our lives diverged. He would have inherited memories of the very same childhood from which I inherited mine, including a memory in which that visit to the Empire State Building with my grandfather would be represented from the perspective of the same six-year-old who I so vividly remember being. To him, as to me, that memory would represent "my visit to the Empire State Building with Grandpa", and we would thereby think of one and the same child as "me".

Yet the reasoning by which I have now explained our sharing a childhood also leads to the conclusion that he would not have been me, and so I could not have been him. For although he and I could think of the same six-year-old as "me", we are not similarly related to one another. I can't look back on anything that happened to him after our lives diverged, and I can't look forward to anything that will happen to him in the future—not, at least, in the way that would make him "me" to me.

Of course, nothing actually happened or actually will happen to him after the point of our imagined divergence, since he never came into existence, to begin with. I'm tempted to say that if he *had* come into existence, then I *would* be able to remember his past and look forward to his future. Certainly, that other David Velleman would be able to. But the question is whether his remembering his past and anticipating his future would amount to my remembering and anticipating mine.

I'm trying to figure out whether I have anything to regret about not having become a dancer, and the emotion of regret presupposes an unrealized possibility. Is there an unrealized possibility in which I became a dancer, even though my present use of "I" and "me" cannot refer to the dancer who would have existed in that case?

Here is something I might be able to regret: I might have been a child who would become a dancer. After all, I really was that child who dreamed of becoming a dancer. Since he might have become one, and I was him, I might have been a child who would become one. Right?

I'm not sure. A child who would become a dancer may not be the child I remember being. The only child I can remember being is the child who was discouraged from studying dance and ended up as a philosophy professor instead. Of course, he *might* have become a dancer. But if he had, the one remembering him now would be the long-retired dancer, not the soon-to-retire philosopher. Then again, how can the two of us—the real philosopher and the nonexistent dancer—share a childhood if neither can remember being the child who would become the other? I'm confused.

No, I can sort this out. It's not that I *might have been* a child who *became* a dancer; rather, I *was* a child who *might have become* a dancer. That child whose dream of dancing might have been fulfilled but wasn't—that child was me.

Here's something I can regret. I can regret not having put my eight-year-old foot down when discouraged from continuing with dance classes. That foot was mine, because the eight-year-old was me. What I cannot regret is not having the present life that he could have had. Or, rather, I can regret it only vicariously, on his behalf, as his unrealized future. That projected regret would be the natural correlative to the childish aspirations that I discovered myself still harboring in my forties—unrealistically, since they were for a future that was already foregone. Responding to those vestigial aspirations with frankly vicarious regret would make sense.

Both kinds of regret—for what I didn't do as a child, and what *he* never became in *his* future—naturally fade as he recedes into the past. If regret were instead proportional to the discrepancy between my present life and the lives my earlier self might have lived, it would increase as time passed and the discrepancy grew. Some people regret a missed opportunity more and more as its unrealized returns increase in their imaginations. (How much those shares of Apple Computer would have been worth today!)

As far as I'm concerned, though, it's not just too late to realize those returns; it's too late to regard the person who would have realized them as me. The life of a dancer might have been a possibility for me at one time, but it isn't a possibility any more, and not only in the sense that it can't be my future: it couldn't even have been my past. There is no point in comparing my story with other stories that, as of now, couldn't have been mine.

5

Aspiring to Authorship

What matters most to me about my life story, in any case, is that I get to write it. I don't like to think that I am just performing a script handed to me by history. I prefer to think of myself as the scriptwriter, inventing my life as I live it, *by* living it.

Inventing my life would require my future to be blank, like the next page of a work-in-progress. The story thus far may limit what I can coherently write on that page, as it does for any writer, but there must be more than one thing I can write.

There do seem to be many possible additions at most junctures; otherwise, I would never have aspired to be the author my life, in the first place. Yet I worry that what looks like a blank page is already written over in invisible ink that I am merely bringing to light.

Some people have a different worry: that they are cogs in a universal clockwork that has been winding down since the beginning of time under inexorable laws of nature. Their worry is that the cosmic mechanism will make it impossible for them to do anything other than what has been destined for them since the beginning of time.

But even if that worry is unwarranted, because more than one course is *possible* for me to take in the future, I still worry that one of those possible courses is already the one that I am *actually* going to take, though God knows what it is. "God knows what it is"—exactly! So long as God could know my future, I am merely discovering it instead of inventing it, catching up with His or Her greater knowledge. I'd like to think that I can make up a life that would surprise even God.

Hubris? I don't think so; I'm just describing what it's like to make a decision. For when I decide to do something, I seem to be making it the case that I'm going to do it. I couldn't be making it the case if it already was the case before I decided; but if it wasn't already the case, then God couldn't have known it—not because of any lack of foresight on His or Her part but because of there being no fact to know. I seem to be creating a fact where there previously was none. Unless there are gaps in the future-tense facts, to be filled in by my decisions, it would rather seem like hubris to claim that I make decisions at all.

Still, I'm puzzled by the notion of gaps in the facts. Surely, what was true this morning in the present tense ("I'm going to the office today") must have been true last night in the future tense ("I will go to the office tomorrow"). Similarly, what I am going to do this afternoon must already have been the topic of future-tense truths this morning. There was already a fact of the matter as to whether I was going to exercise at the gym after work. So why did it seem this morning as if the question was still open?

The question seemed open because I seemed to have a choice between two descriptions of the future—"I will go to the gym this afternoon" or "I won't go to the gym" —either of which I could make true by making a decision with that description as its content. The problem is that one of these descriptions was already false, since there was already a fact of the matter. So how could there have been a choice for me to make? The antecedent existence of a fact seems to have preempted my decision by ruling out one of the alternatives even before I considered it. Why bother considering whether to visit the gym this afternoon if it was already a fact that I wouldn't?

The problem is that *deciding* what *to* do seems to consist in *describing* what I *will* do. In making my decision this morning, I thought either "I'll go to the gym" or "I won't go to the gym". Because one of those descriptions was already false, one of the decisions seems to have been ruled out in advance.

Yet if thinking either description would amount to making a decision, it would lead me to act accordingly. The thought "I'll go to the gym" would lead me to go, and the contrary thought, contrariwise. So I was never at risk of thinking something false. For if I wasn't going to exercise this afternoon, the reason must have been that I wasn't about to think I would, which still could not have made it incorrect to think so, given that thinking so would have amounted to deciding to exercise, which would have led me to exercise, after all. Either thought, being a decision, would have been self-fulfilling, making itself come true.

Not all by itself, of course. A decision to go to the gym would get me to go only because I also have good reasons for exercising, which will weigh with me later on, when it's time to act on that decision. But those reasons aren't specific to today: I can put off exercise until tomorrow and end up being just as fit—which is exactly what I'm likely to think at 5:00, when I'm tired and the stink of the locker room looms nearer. If I keep putting it off day after day, though, I'll get out of shape, and getting back into shape will be a struggle—which will become a progressively stronger deterrent to getting started again. So I shouldn't let myself deteriorate to that point. But if I haven't already reached that point, one more day won't make much difference; and even if I have, it won't make much difference if I take one more day off before facing the struggle of getting back into shape.

Clearly, leaving the decision until 5:00 is a recipe for never getting myself to exercise at all. That's why I decided this morning, "I'll go to the gym this afternoon," relying on that thought to turn my feet in the right direction at 5:00.

Not every self-fulling thought is a decision, though. If I worry that I'll lie awake all night, that worry will keep me awake, but it won't be a decision to suffer insomnia. Maybe the difference is that I won't realize I'm being kept awake by that very thought, whereas in thinking "I'll go to the gym", I expected to go as a result of thereby deciding to. (I wasn't deciding to do something that I thought I was already going to do anyway, whether or not I decided to.) So my thought not only *was* self-fulfilling but implicitly regarded itself *as* self-fulfilling.

Yet even if a thought regards itself as self-fulfilling—"I can't sleep (because I'm thinking so)"—I still haven't made a decision. What is the remaining difference?

The difference is that insomnia doesn't leave me the option of thinking otherwise. Any thought of sleep—even the thought that I *will* sleep—triggers my fear of insomnia, which keeps me awake; and any attempt to avoid thinking of sleep only brings it to mind. No matter how I barricade my mind against the sleep-destroying thought of sleep, it slips right in. By contrast, my thought about going to the gym was optional. I thought it because of wanting to make it true, and I could have thought the opposite if I had wanted the opposite, given that I could make either one true by thinking it. In short, a decision is an optional self-fulfilling thought that regards itself as such.

Such thoughts are like assumptions. At first, I had no evidence for one over the other, and I could have adopted either one, simply assuming it was true. No matter which one I assumed, it would have thereupon been favored by evidence—the fact that I had assumed it plus the fact of its being self-fulfilling—and so it would have become more than an assumption, a well-supported belief. Not knowing at first whether I would exercise this afternoon, I could instantly come to know that I would or that I wouldn't, just by assuming one or the other.

I've been avoiding the hardest question: Why should I have thought that my assumption as to whether I'd exercise this afternoon would actually make itself true? As the saying goes, thinking doesn't make it so.

It would certainly be convenient if such an assumption were self-fulfilling and I had evidence that it was. It's useful to know in the morning whether I'll go to the gym in the afternoon. If I will go, I should pack my exercise gear in my backpack and, at noon, eat a light lunch. If I won't go, then I needn't round up my gear, but I should clear my calendar for tomorrow afternoon so that I can make up for the exercise I will have shirked today. Knowing whether I'll go to the gym today would enable me to make the necessary preparations and would spare me from making unnecessary preparations for the alternative.

I could actually have that ability if I generally tended to fulfill assumptions of that sort and if I had evidence of that tendency. Given reliable evidence of tending to fulfill assumptions that regard themselves as self-fulfilling, I could entertain a range of future activities each of which I could think I would undertake (or not), confident of thereby adding to any inclination I already had for undertaking it (or not). Of course, there would be many things that I was simply unable to do, and others that I would be overwhelmingly averse to doing even if I assumed that I would do them because of so assuming. Those things, I'd have to avoid assuming I'd do. But I would still have many alternatives, things that I could confidently assume I'd do because of so assuming, given evidence of tending to bear out such assumptions. I want to have that tendency and evidence that I have it.

Hold on. The evidence is already within reach: I can get it just by carrying out my attempted decisions—that is, my purportedly self-fulfilling assumptions about what I'll do. By bearing out those assumptions, I can give myself the desired evidence of tending to bear them out—evidence, in short, of my stick-to-it-iveness, or constancy. So my desire for that evidence is a motive for carrying out my decisions: it already *is* my constancy.

Nah, that's cheating—isn't it? Usually, if I try to produce evidence for some conclusion about myself, I'm putting on a false front, feigning friendliness to people I dislike, miming attentiveness to a speaker whose words are going in one ear and out the other. Isn't there some fakery involved in fulfilling purportedly self-fulfilling assumptions about myself in order to give myself evidence on which to base such assumptions in the future? The only difference, it seems, is that when I fulfill my own assumptions about what I'll do, the person I'm trying to fool is me.

Am I really trying to fool myself, though? The conclusion for which I'm trying to produce evidence is that I'm inclined to fulfill purportedly self-fulfilling assumptions about myself; and wanting to produce that evidence just *is* an inclination of the sort for which I'm trying to produce that evidence.

The comparison to cases of fakery isn't fair. Wanting to be considered friendly is a motive only for acting friendly, which is not enough for genuine friendliness: being friendly also requires particular feelings behind the friendly behavior, and a desire merely to seem friendly isn't one of them. But constancy is nothing more than an inclination to stick to one's plans, even if only because of wanting evidence that one is so inclined.

In that respect, constancy is a bit like trustworthiness. I'm inclined to keep my promises in order to prove that I keep them, and similarly, I'm inclined to stick to my plans in order to prove that I stick to them. True, the motive for proving myself trustworthy cannot be the whole of trustworthiness, since it doesn't operate in the case of promises I could break without being found out. But I am bound to find out if I haven't stuck to a plan, and so the motive for displaying constancy really can be all there is to it.

I admit there are other differences between plans and promises. If I promise a friend to be at the gym this afternoon, my friend can excuse me from keeping the promise, and then my reputation for trustworthiness won't suffer when I don't show up. Indeed, my reputation will remain intact even if I renew the promise day after day and never show up, provided that I've been excused every time. Excusing myself from sticking to a plan, however, would amount to changing my mind; and although I can occasionally change my mind and still make reliable plans, I can't excuse myself repeatedly without undermining my basis for planning altogether. The friend who has repeatedly excused me from my promises in the past has no reason for hesitating to rely on the next promise I give (though he has deprived himself of a chance to gather evidence for relying on it). If I repeatedly change my plans, however, I will no longer be able to rely on them at all, and they will lose their practical value.

Sometimes the need to rely on a plan is especially urgent—for example, when I postpone a vital chore to the last minute on the assumption that I really will do it then. In an evening of binge-watching a TV series, I may be depending on the assumption that I really will wash the dishes before going to bed. In that case, I can signal to myself that my assumption is one I especially need to count on, so that I will be especially motivated to fulfill it, so that I have a basis for counting on assumptions that I especially need to count on. The signal may simply be the word "really" plus a bit of emphasis, as in "I really *will* do the dishes before bed", which makes defaulting on the assumption especially costly by undermining the evidence supporting assumptions to which I've added that signal because of especially needing to count on them. If I undermine that evidence, I may have to give up binge-watching TV.

There can also be unintentional cues that undermine the value of such assumptions as evidence, by canceling the costs of falsifying them. One such cue is the label "New Year's resolution". I can treat New Year's resolutions differently from all of my other plans and resolutions, precisely because I can put them in a separate category, namely, "New Year's resolutions". Whether I keep my New Year's resolutions needn't reflect on whether I tend to do what I resolve to do in general; it reflects only on whether I do what I New-Year's-resolve to do. Even if I break these resolutions, which I make only once a year, my basis for relying on resolutions in general remains intact. That's why I so frequently default on New Year's resolutions: they give me no particular reason to carry them out. (I stopped making them long ago.)

ᴄℓ~

How did I get to this point? I started out with the worry that truly authoring my future would require it to be a blank page waiting to be filled in with my decisions. If it already was filled in, even in invisible ink, my role as author would have been preempted—or so I thought. But now I see that my authorship cannot be so easily preempted, because the future-tense facts are sometimes dependent on what I think they will be, so that I can think what I like about them without going wrong.

Sometimes the openness of the future is out in public. I go to a restaurant for lunch, the waiter asks "What will you have?", and we both know I can reply with anything on the menu. Maybe I reply, "I'll have a club sandwich," assuming that if I say I'll have a club sandwich, then that's what I'll get and consequently what I'll have. My statement is self-fulfilling, and so I could have said with equal truth that I'd have something else.

Now, if the waiter replies, "We're all out of turkey," I might add, "Then I guess I won't have a club sandwich," indicating that I was trying to speak the truth. (I won't add, "Then don't bring me one," as if my initial utterance was meant as a command.) But if no such bad news is forthcoming, then I'll know that I will indeed have a club sandwich. I'll also know that I was going to have a club sandwich all along, since what's true then must already have been true the previous day, the previous week, and so on, back to the beginning of time. Does that knowledge lead me to think that I would have been mistaken to say, "I'll have the meat loaf"? Of course not. I'll have whatever I say, and so I can say whatever I like without making a mistake.

If the waiter is psychic and already knows what I'll have for lunch, he might *tell* me what I'll have, by saying, "You're going to have a club sandwich," perhaps in a portentous monotone, with a mystical look in his eyes. I might of course take him for a tyrannical type, issuing a command—in which case, I'd slip out and seek lunch elsewhere. If I know that he's making a prediction, however, I might be tempted to contradict him, so as to prove that I'm not so predictable. Despite preferring a club sandwich, I might perversely want to say, "No, I'll have the meat loaf," so that he would have to bring me meat loaf and stop pretending to be psychic.

But if he really *is* psychic, then his prediction must be true. And if I *know* that he's psychic, and that his prediction is therefore true, then I must know that I'm going to order a club sandwich. Can't that knowledge deprive me of a choice in the matter? How can I decide what to have for lunch if I've already been authoritatively informed that I'm going to have a club sandwich?

Well, as a bona fide psychic, the waiter must know that if he says I'll have a club sandwich, I won't contradict him; otherwise he'd have to bring me something else, and his prediction would turn out to have been false. He must also know I'm confident that I'll have something other than a club sandwich if I say so. So he must know that the only reason I'm not going to contradict him is that I prefer the club sandwich (and harbor no hostility to psychics). Otherwise, he wouldn't have predicted the club sandwich, in the first place. So it must be the case that I prefer a club sandwich.

That's why I don't contradict him: I really do prefer the club sandwich, as he must have known in making his prediction. So when he says, "You'll have a club sandwich," I respond, "That's just what I was about to say!" because I really was about to say it, given my preference. The reason I don't say, "I'll have the meat loaf," isn't that it would be false; it's that I don't want to, because I prefer a club sandwich.

Similarly, the fact that I'll go to the gym after work cannot preempt my decision about whether to go. Even if I could have read the story of the day in advance and it said, "At 5:00 I'll go to the gym," I wouldn't have thought, "Well, then, I guess I'll be going to the gym this afternoon: better gather my gear," as if deferring to the authority of what was written. Rather, I would have thought, "That's just what I was about to think," and then I would have thought it, because I wanted it to be true, knowing that I could with equal confidence think the opposite. That thought would still be a decision on my part despite its having been anticipated. And if I read the same statement at 5:00 pm, I'd think, "Darn right I'm going to the gym: that's what I decided this morning, and I'm going to stick to it." In neither case would I be deferring to what was written; in both cases, my thoughts would still be optional, since the opposite thoughts would be equally true.

In reality, of course, I didn't need to read my future, because I could tell it just by deciding. But a pre-written story of my day would not have supplanted me in the role of author. It would have been a story of my doing things because of first assuming I'd do them, where I wouldn't have done them if I hadn't assumed so. That would be the story of me authoring my future by making assumptions about it at will. It would certify my authorship, not disprove it.

6

Making Things Happen

Is that enough—being the author of my life? It certainly doesn't change the fact that my actions are determined by earlier events, which were determined by even earlier events, ultimately dating back to the time before I was born.

Even if I can correctly assume whatever I want about my forthcoming actions, prior events will have determined what I want, which will determine what I assume, which will determine what I do. If my trip to the gym is prompted by the assumption I'll go, and the assumption is caused by a desire to avoid procrastinating, which arises from concern for my health, which is due to my inborn prudence and wholesome upbringing, which I owe to my parents' chromosomes and *their* upbringing, and so on … well, then, perhaps I won't be entitled to congratulate myself on the distance I swim or the weight I lift. Then again, maybe I shouldn't have worried about blaming myself for going to seed if I didn't exercise. For how can I be responsible for anything that happens unless I make it happen? And how can I make anything happen if everything that happens is caused by facts and events other than me?

I don't even have to look outside myself to find causes that seem to challenge my pretensions of making things happen. The immediate causes for my going to the gym include workings of my body and mind—chromosomes, prudence, concern, desire, assumption—but where am *I* in that sequence? I feel responsible for what I do when I feel as if I'm intervening in the world from outside the web of worldly causes, like a deus ex machina. Yet my actions are controlled by strands of that web, and those strands are being pulled by things that happen *in* me or are part *of* me, but not by *me*, myself.

~~~

I don't deny that movements caused in that way can still be my doing in some sense or other. When nerve impulses briefly trigger the muscles in my eyelids, I blink; when fever or fear causes my body to shake, I shiver; when a surprise causes a sudden contraction of my diaphragm, I gasp. These causes go proxy for me, in the sense that whatever they cause, I do.

Yes, but my doing those things doesn't entail being responsible for doing them. I can't be credited or blamed for my blinks, shivers, and gasps. *I* don't make them happen, or at least not in the way that would make me responsible for them. But when I swim an extra ten laps or lift an extra ten pounds, I am producing those achievements in such a way as to deserve credit for them. And yet they are caused by muscle contractions that are caused by nerve impulses that are due to all of those causes I mentioned earlier, which appear to crowd me out of being the cause.

I'm forgetting something.

By now I know that I am a train of momentary sub jects who can think of one another as "me" in virtue of being linked by memory. Yet I've just mentioned some things—nerve impulses, muscle contractions—in which there isn't a subject at all, because they don't embody a point of view, like attitudes or feelings or experiences. They aren't subjective phenomena, in other words, and so they have no subject in the relevant sense. If my efficacy must emanate from *me*, I should be looking for it in causes of which I am the subject—my desire to stay fit, for example, or my assumption that I'll exercise. Surely, *their* efficacy can amount to *my* efficacy.

But here's a problem. When I think of that desire and assumption as causing my turn toward the gym, I am not thinking from the perspective of their subject. Rather, I have stepped back from them and made them objects of reflection, observing them as if from a distance. And then they once again seem to supplant me as cause. There they are, motivating my behavior, and here I am, passively reflecting on them. I seem to be sidelined, out of the action. How do I get into the act?

Sometimes I'm not at all distanced from such causes of my behavior, because I'm being carried along by a motivational tide in which I'm fully immersed. I may not recognize my motivating anger until I find myself shouting at someone. I may not recognize my diffidence until I notice myself avoiding someone's eye, or my hunger until I'm already standing at the open door of the fridge. Yet those cases of unreflective behavior are hardly paradigms of personal efficacy, in which I'm clearly responsible for my behavior; on the contrary, they are cases in which I seem to have been carried along by my anger, diffidence, or hunger. The times when it feels like me producing a shout, and not just my anger erupting, are the times when I recognize the anger first and then decide to express it.

That's odd. I thought being the cause of my behavior would consist in being the subject of the motives behind it; yet I actually seem to be causing it when I'm reflectively aware of my motives, occupying a position that I described a moment earlier as passive. First I said that my motives *can't* stand in for me when I'm reflecting on them, because I'm standing apart from them in order to reflect; and then I said that reflective awareness of them is what seems to get me into the act.

Could it be that reflection isn't as passive as I thought? After all, stepping back into a perspective of detached reflection is itself an action—a mental action. I am rarely aware of a motive behind it, because it requires little or no effort, but there must be one.

Granted. But that's just another motive. It won't implicate me in causing my behavior if I can take up a perspective of reflective detachment from it as well.

Granted again. But now I see that I can't. When I try to imagine stepping back from my motive for reflecting, I realize that I haven't really stepped back. In reflecting on that motive, I am still acting out of it, and so I am less than completely detached from it. Maybe that motive—a motive from which I cannot fully step back—is the one whose efficacy is mine.

I just reread that last paragraph and barely understood it. If only there was a concrete example of what I have in mind ....

Come to think of it, I've seen an example in ballet class. The mirrors on the studio walls show me a dancer whom I can sometimes watch with critical detachment. Music and muscle memory carry my body through a step as I look on, watching myself as if from a distance. I can *see* that dancer without having the sense of *being* him. If I make eye contact with my reflection, however, the distance instantly collapses: those eyes in the mirror are obviously the eyes through which I'm seeing them, and so I am aware of being the subject as well as the object of that gaze. In fact, the distance can collapse even in the absence of eye contact: it collapses as soon as I perform a

step for my own inspection in the mirror. When performing a step out of a desire to see it, I am not watching it from a distance, because what I'm seeing is an expression of the same desire that is moving me to watch. The figure in the mirror is dancing in order to observe himself dancing, and so I can't gain distance from him by retreating to the position of observer. Seeing him is no longer detachable from the sense of being him.

The desire to watch myself execute a step is not the only motive behind its execution. I also want to follow the teacher's instructions and to express the spirit of the music. The desire to see how I'm doing is an additional motive that reinforces and modifies the others. But those other motives might have actuated my body through muscle memory and musicianship alone, leaving me to watch from the sidelines. In this case, however, the desire to see myself execute the step is implicated in causing the action I see, and it implicates me as well. Adopting the perspective of the observer doesn't distance me from the perspective of the observed.

Mirrors may not be necessary to produce this effect. Whenever I try to do something well in the sense of displaying good form—serving a tennis ball, thanking a host —I am observing my performance and comparing it with a conception of what would count as good form, adjusting my performance to match that conception. Sometimes, of course, I toss off a thank-you out of reflexive courtesy without having to aim at doing it well, because I can rely on long-standing habit and still end up doing it pretty well. I am happy to give my parents and teachers the credit for inculcating the habit operative in that case. But when I try to conform what I'm doing to my conception of how to do it well, the manner in which I do it is shaped by a desire to see myself living up to that conception: I am acting partly from the motives of self-critical observer, though without the help of a mirror. I probably can't claim credit for my conception of how properly to thank a host, but I cannot help regarding the resulting behavior as my own doing, because I can't gain distance from it by retreating to the observer's standpoint.

These examples have helped—a bit—but they are complex and confined to special circumstances. I need to see whether they can illuminate my sense of personal efficacy more generally.

In just a moment, I'll get up for a drink of water. Or maybe I'll just get up to stretch my legs. But here's something I won't do: I won't put myself in a position of having to ask, "Why am I standing up? Where am I going?" I generally don't start doing anything without at least being prepared to find myself doing it; and the reason is that I generally want to know what I'm up to—a desire that is perhaps the most general motive for reflecting.

Sometimes I start walking up the stairs only to realize, mid-flight, that I don't know what I'm doing. I know that I'm walking upstairs, of course, but why? Am I going to fetch my slippers? To lie down for a nap? I stop to think.

Strangely, I can't answer my question by proceeding up the stairs to see what I do at the top. Whatever I was doing, I'm no longer doing it. What I'm now doing is this: trying to figure out what I *was* doing when I started. Climbing the rest of the way in order to figure out what I was doing is certainly not what I was doing, and so it would necessarily fail.

Why do I stop when I realize that I don't know what I'm doing? The reason, obviously, is that not knowing what I'm doing is a very disturbing sort of confusion— more disturbing than other sorts of confusion, because it's about my own behavior here and now. At this point on the stairs, I prefer not to do anything until I know what it's going to be, so that I'll know what I'm doing as I do it.

The necessary preparation doesn't always require a pause for reflection. For example, I usually don't say anything unless I'm prepared to hear myself say it, and yet I don't formulate the words first, silently, before going on to articulate them. When I know what I'm going to say, it's not because I've already said it to myself. Sometimes I follow an utterance with "That's not what I meant to say," but not because I've made a mistake in performing a prepared speech. "That's not what I meant to say" usually means that, having heard myself say something, I find it inadequate to a thought that I hadn't yet formulated in words, not even to myself. It strikes me as inadequate because I'm dissatisfied with what I've found myself saying.

Sometimes, especially while waiting my turn to speak, I have a distinct sense of already knowing what I'm going to say. But what does this knowledge consist in? I may have thought of a key word or phrase that I intend to arrive at in the course of speaking, but often I've thought of no words at all. My knowing what I'm going to say seems to be the sort of *knowing* something that consists in *being able to say* what it is. But being able to say what I'm going to say is just the ability to say it, the very utterance of which I'm claiming foreknowledge. When someone interrupts me, apologizes, and asks, "What were you going to say?" I just resume my utterance from the beginning.

The sense of knowing what I'm going to say is thus no more than a feeling of being prepared to say something that I'm prepared to hear myself say, though I haven't yet formulated it and hence don't exactly know what it is, except in the sense of being able to say it without disconcerting myself. There is, in me, a preconscious speaker whose words become conscious precisely by being spoken; and I generally trust him to say what I, having heard it, will agree to have meant. If he lets me down, I immediately interrupt, in the same way as I stop climbing the stairs if I don't know why.

So I am not just speaking for the ears of my conversational partners; I am also aware that I will hear what I say, and I am hoping to make sense and seem sensible to all of my hearers, including myself—especially myself, since my own satisfaction with what I say is of special importance to me. Trying to make sense to myself is not something I do consciously. Consciously, I just let the words come out, trusting that they'll usually be something I mean and, failing that, can easily be revised or retracted. The only conscious control I exercise is supervisory.

Unconsciously, though, I am inhibited by the knowledge of being supervised. I speak without forethought but in unconscious anticipation of afterthought. Just as I unconsciously avoid bumping into chairs and tables when I walk, I unconsciously avoid arousing my own dissatisfaction when I talk. I devote no attention to avoiding such mishaps, but it's no accident that I generally manage to avoid them.

When I bring these reflections to bear on my other activities, I find that many of them are equally free of forethought. Sitting here at my desk, I occasionally get up and pace the hall, or check my email, or stare out the window, or do some other thing that I already know I won't balk at finding myself doing. I don't decide to do one rather than another, unless by "decide" I mean "do without fear of balking", which doesn't involve any positive decision.

More than passive supervision is needed, however, when it comes to actions that are not habitual in the present context. I am not prepared to find myself doing them at the moment, and so I need to prepare myself, by thinking of them in advance, lest I end up not knowing what I'm up to. This afternoon I won't leave for the gym until a moment after I've assumed that I'll leave momentarily. Unlike pacing the hall, leaving for the day is not the sort of thing that I'm continually ready to see myself doing. I already know that I'll leave at some point, but I'm not prepared to see myself leaving at any moment. It's the sort of thing that I will need to have thought I'm going to do next, lest I risk wondering what I'm doing. Rather than mystify myself in that way, I'll make the final update to my plan: "Now I'll leave for the gym".

And then, because leaving for the gym is what I've pre-pared myself to find myself doing next, I will get up and leave, so as not to end up wondering why I'm *not* leaving. The thought of leaving will thus be self-fulfilling. In fact, that's how I knew the plan would be self-fulfilling when I adopted it this morning. I knew that the final update, "Now I'll leave", would prompt me to leave because of just having thought so.

This sort of deliberate action feels different from the ones that I merely supervise. The difference between them resembles the difference between the ballet steps I merely see myself take and the steps I perform for my own inspection.

When I find myself pacing the hall, as I often do out of restlessness, it feels as if the restlessness has set me in motion. *I* didn't really initiate the activity; it was initiated by restlessness itself, though I wasn't surprised or puzzled by what I found myself doing. My restlessness was like the muscle memory behind the ballet steps that I see in the mirror when watching as if from a distance. When I leave for the gym, however, what sets me going is the thought "Now I'll leave", plus my motive for making and bearing out that assumption. That motive seems to implicate me in causing my behavior to an extent that restlessness did not. And now I think I know why: it's the motive of reflection, which is like the motive for demonstrating a step for myself in the ballet studio mirror.

If I wonder why I'm pacing the hall, the answer will be that I'm restless; if instead of answering that question, I go on to wonder why I'm asking it—why I'm wondering why I'm pacing the hall—the answer will be that I want to know what I'm up to. Answering either question will entail reflecting on what I'm doing—either pacing or wondering why. But the first question will be about my motive for pacing, which I can consider from a perspective of detached reflection; the second question will be about my motive for reflecting, from which I cannot detach myself in the same way. In order to step back from my motive for reflecting, I have to reflect on it, and then it is still behind the lens of self-investigation, not fully objectified because I am its subject. I can never see my reflecting self without retaining the sense of being him.

That motive of reflection—wanting to know what I'm up to—is also the motive that subliminally deters me from doing anything I'm not prepared to find myself doing, then moves me to prepare myself by assuming I'll do something, and then switches from restraining to reinforcing

my other motives for doing it. In short, it's my motive for making and acting on immediate decisions when my next move isn't already obvious. That's why I have the sense of causing my behavior when I act on an immediate decision: I am inextricably implicated in causing that behavior because I can't dissociate myself from one of its motives. My making things happen, in other words, is a matter of not being able to attain any distance from a motive that's making it happen.

It seems like a strange motive to go proxy for me in making things happen. Then again, it's an instance of a motive that has been at work in me almost since birth: my innate drive to make sense of the world, of which I am an especially salient element.

I'm not usually conscious of that drive in myself, but I remember seeing it at work in my children from the first moment their fists reached their mouths. From then on, they spent almost every waking moment experimenting with parts of the world to see how it works. I no longer live in constant service to that motive, but only because I already know how things work by and large. I quickly return to its service whenever the world throws me a curve.

The newborn's experience of a coincidence between a sensation in its mouth and a sensation in its fist is probably like the experience of a cat catching its own tail. The cat doesn't think, "Oh! That's my tail." That thought would require the cat to know it's a creature seeing its own tail, and it doesn't know it is one of the creatures in the world, a creature that it can see and feel and that is also the one thereby seeing and feeling it. A child eventually does have that realization, whereupon it is ready to master the first-person pronoun.

Before that age, our daughter would hold up her arms to us and say, "Pick you up!", which was what she usually heard just before being picked up. In order to master "Pick *me* up", she had to realize that she was presenting

us with a child to be picked up—in fact, a child wanting to be understood by us as wanting to be picked up. And at that point, she must have known that she was one of the world's creatures, and that she'd better know what that creature is up to. She was then only a step away from realizing that she could be sure of knowing what it is up to by not getting up to anything that she doesn't already know about, either because it's something she usually does or because it's something she assumes she'll do as a result of this very assumption.

I suspect that the willfulness of her "terrible twos" was the result of trial and error at wielding her newly acquired will—the newly acquired capacity to make and act on immediate decisions. Having thought, "I am *not* going to put on my shoes," she didn't yet appreciate that this thought was still optional, because she'd be equally correct to think, "Now I'll put them on." (On our part, we didn't at first appreciate that the most effective way of getting her to cooperate was to say, "Now we'll put on our shoes," hoping to enlist her in an assumption that would become self-fulfilling.)

The times when my anger erupts in shouting at someone are the times when I am liable to ask myself, "What am I doing?" If no answer occurs to me, I'll lower my voice. Even if I immediately recognize why I'm shouting, a subtle change comes over my behavior. Now I have to decide whether to continue expressing my anger or to pipe down. And then I will be in control rather than carried away. I will have "composed" myself, at least to the extent of being, in my own eyes, a person shouting in anger, if not a person already exerting self-control. Either conception of myself will be a "composition" motivated by the desire to know what I'm up to, which will then motivate me to enact it, ensconced in the perspective of its cause.

Do I deserve to be blamed for shouting, or praised for lowering my voice? I still haven't figured that out.

I've figured out why I have the sense of causing one or the other. Indeed, I've figured out why I feel like a deus ex machina when I do so. First I feel there is no fact about what I'll do next ("Will I go on shouting or not?") because I'd be correct in assuming I'll do either one. Then I assume that I'll do one of them, prompting myself to do it partly out of a motive from which I cannot step back. I seem to be a force creating a fact where there was none before.

Of course, I am not identical with that force; I am merely unable to escape the perspective of its subject. And I cannot create a previously nonexistent fact. So this explanation falls far short of casting me as a genuine deus ex machina. And it's only when I seem to occupy that exalted position that I feel fully responsible for what I do.

So am I really responsible?

Although I've figured out a fair amount about being me, this is something I don't yet understand. Maybe I need to revise my conception of what it takes to deserve credit or blame—a conception that was formed, after all, under an illusion of divinity. Maybe I can then hold myself responsible for things under different standards of what responsibility requires. Or maybe my standards of responsibility are fine just as they are. Or maybe responsibility is an illusion I ought to dispel. I just don't know.

7

Wanting to Be Loved

I want to be loved for being me.

Not for being David Velleman. He *is* lovable, I hope, but what's lovable about him is not that he's David Velleman.

How about this: I want to be loved for what I am *like*.

No, that's something I don't want. What I am like has changed over the course of my life and continues to change. I used to be a gregarious optimist and I've gradually become an introverted curmudgeon. Mercifully, there are people whose love has survived my evolution from good company to pain in the ass. Their love sees something constant under the changes.

I do worry that under those changes, there is nothing about me that is worthy of love; and I don't really want to be loved while being unworthy. Rather, I hope that something about me is worthy of love and that I will be loved for it. When I say that I want to be loved for being me, I mean that I want to be loved for that better self which I hope—even dare to believe—lies beneath whatever is unlovable about me. Where is that better self?

When I focus my mind on what I hope to be valued for, I don't attend to any particular qualities or accomplishments; I just sit by myself and entertain a vivid awareness of myself. The self that I have to offer to others as an object of love is the self that is present to me in solitude, when I am not just *by* myself but *with* myself, keeping myself company.

Sometimes I can't stand my own company, and then I don't feel worth loving. The times when I can't stand being with myself are the times when I've been mean or dishonest or conceited—in short, when I've been bad. Could it be that I want to be loved for being *good*?

Well, what is present to me in solitude? All that's present to me, it seems, is the local scene as experienced from my perspective plus a person *in* that scene whose perspective it is. At the moment, that person is being neither charming nor brilliant, and yet such moments of quiet, reflective idleness are the moments when I am most aware of that in me which I hope others will love, since they are the moments when I am just being me, not under any particular guise. And how could just being me entail being worthy of love? As I've been saying all along, "me" is just a pronoun that points to the subject currently using it and to past and future subjects from whom he can receive, and to whom he can send, uses of the same pronoun. If being me is nothing more than being the referent of a pronoun, it seems too insubstantial to support the weight of goodness, much less the weight of love.

But maybe being me is more than that. Precisely because the pronoun refers to its user, it can refer only to creatures that are capable of using it. A cat can be called "him" or "her" or "it"—even "you"—but never "me". The pronoun can be used only by, and hence only for, a creature aware of itself *as* a creature thereby referring to itself.

I vividly remember lying in bed as a child and saying to myself, with a sense of wonder, "I am me; me am I." These statements expressed something elemental, mangled syntax and all: they expressed the realization that there is a creature in the world who I am, whom I call "me".

I marveled at the fact of being that self-aware creature. How lucky can you get! This relation that I as subject bear to myself as object is what becomes salient to me in solitude. Could there be anything good—anything worth loving, even—in this relation between the subject called "I" and the object called "me"?

That relation, I've recently concluded, is the site of my making things happen. As a hearer of my own speech to whom I'm subliminally trying to make sense, or a viewer of my behavior subliminally guarding against surprises, or a planner seeking to maintain visibility into my future, or the executor of plans and decisions—in all of these roles, I occupy a perspective of reflection from which there is no stepping back. The motive informing that perspective, the desire to know what I am up to, is therefore the force whose impact on the world is most truly mine.

And here's the thing: from that perspective, I view the object of my reflection as just a person—the particular person to whom the perspective belongs, of course, but a creature that must be understood *as* a person, who does things of the kinds that people generally do, out of thoughts and feelings and habits and traits that people generally have. The vocabulary available to me for describing what I'm up to, and the common sense available for understanding it, are the same resources I use to describe or understand anyone. From that inescapable perspective of reflection, I am a person whose behavior must be grasped in the same terms as any person's behavior.

Apparently, then, my personal efficacy arises from a duality in me that makes me just another person in my own eyes. That perspective on myself is not sufficient by itself to make me good, but perhaps it is the beginning of goodness—for it entails regarding myself as just one person in a world of persons. It thus initiates a train of thought that eventually leads me to recognize the symmetry between my treatment of others and their treatment of me.

Could the Golden Rule be inscribed in the very structure of being me?

But now I am truly blocked from going further in this introspective vein. In order to understand how seeing myself as one person among others might make me good, and perhaps even worthy of love, I would have to look beyond myself to my interactions with others. I'd have to learn things that aren't available to solitary reflection. So I'll stop here for now (so I think, and so I stop).

Readings

Harry Frankfurt, *The Importance of What We Care About* (Cambridge: Cambridge University Press, 1998).

Thomas Nagel, *The View from Nowhere* (Oxford: Oxford University Press, 1986).

John Perry, *A Dialog on Personal Identity and Immortality* (Indianapolis: Hackett, 1978).

J. David Velleman, *How We Get Along* (Cambridge: Cambridge University Press, 2009).

J. David Velleman, *Self to Self* (Ann Arbor, MI: Michigan Publishing, 2020), https://doi.org/10.3998/mpub.11654791.

Bernard Williams, *Problems of the Self* (Cambridge: Cambridge University Press, 1973).

Acknowledgments

For comments on earlier versions of *On Being Me*, I am grateful to Linda Wimer Brakel, Michael Bratman, Kitty Bridges, Jennifer Church, Daniela Dover, David V. Johnson, Michelle Kosch, Ted Lawrence, Jessica Moss, Lucy O'Brien, David Owens, David Satran, Matty Silverstein, Sharon Street, Dan Velleman, Paul Velleman, and Susan Wolf. I am especially indebted to Matt Rohal, the philosophy editor at Princeton University Press, for encouragement and guidance. I am also grateful to New York University's Department of Philosophy and the College of Arts and Science for a semester's leave.